Shadow Redwork

with Alex Anderson

24 DESIGNS TO MIX AND MATCH

C&T PUBLISHING

2001 © Alex Anderson
Illustrations 2001 © C&T Publishing, Inc.

Developmental Editor: Liz Aneloski
Technical Editors: Lynn Koolish & Joyce Engels Lytle
Copy Editor: Carol Barrett
Design Direction: Diane Pedersen
Book Designer: Staci Harpole, Cubic Design
Production Assistant: Stephanie Muir
Illustrator: Lee Nelson
Cover & Quilt Photography: Sharon Risedorph
Cover Redwork: Alex Anderson

Published by C&T Publishing, Inc., P.O. Box 1456, Lafayette, California 94549

Attention Teachers:
C&T Publishing, Inc. encourages you to use this book as a text for teaching. Contact us at 800-284-1114 or www.ctpub.com for more information about the C&T Teachers Program.

Trademarked (™) and Registered Trademarked (®) names are used throughout this book. Rather than use the symbols with every occurrence of a trademark and registered trademark name, we are using the names only in an editorial fashion and to the benefit of the owner, with no intention of infringement.

We take great care to ensure that the information included in this book is accurate and presented in good faith, but no warranty is provided nor results guaranteed. Since we have no control over the choice of materials or procedures used, neither the author nor C&T Publishing, Inc. shall have any liability to any person or entity with respect to any loss or damage caused directly or indirectly by the information contained in this book.

Library of Congress Cataloging-in-Publication Data

Anderson, Alex
    Shadow redwork with Alex Anderson : 24 designs to mix & match
    / Alex Anderson.
            p.   cm.
    ISBN 1-57120-156-4
    1. Embroidery--Patterns. 2. Decoration and ornament--Plant forms.
    3. Quilts. 4. Pillows. I. Title.
    TT773 .A633 2001
    746.44'041--dc21
                                        00-010872

Printed in Hong Kong

10 9 8 7 6 5 4 3 2 1

Dedication

To my friend Nancy Sands; your excellent eye, talented hands, and wise spirit are a gift to me.

Acknowledgements

Thank you to Margaret Bender, Pearl Denison, Nancy Sands, Margaret Scott, Patricia Shaw, and Kimberly Watkins. Without your cooperation and gifted hands, this book would have been impossible to produce. Thank you to Anna Pope of Proctor's Framing, Livermore, California. Thank you to Liz Aneloski, Joyce Lytle, Lynn Koolish, Kandy Peterson, and Staci Harpole who caught the excitement of this technique and crunched this book into their already demanding schedules! It was a joy to work with all of you.

Contents

It was a joy to work with all of you.

Introduction

Not too long ago, I was invited to teach on a cruise to the Bahamas (it's a tough job, but someone has to do it). After dancing around the room, promising to snorkel, and agreeing to be seen publicly in a bathing suit, it was time to determine which classes to teach. In addition to my standard classes, hand quilting and stars, I needed a three-hour class appropriate for hand-work. It seemed that redwork was the perfect answer! With a trusty pencil in hand, it was time to draw. The cruise was around Valentines Day, so hearts were the way to go. One thing led to another, and before I knew it little redwork hearts and flowers were taking over my life. The little six-inch patches were with me at volleyball games and on airplanes. I was hooked and found that redwork was the perfect project for a mom on the go or for someone who was simply seeking a fun and relaxing project. The original wallhanging pattern, Redwork Garden, is available at quilt shops and on my web site www.alexandersonquilts.com. My pencil didn't stop drawing when that design was complete. Flowers kept dancing from my brain onto paper. At the same time, I was asked to speak at a Mother's Day luncheon and thought it would be nice to design a special pattern for that occasion—the Nasturtiums Pillow (page 5). I found that adding the lettering behind the redwork design added a wonderful element and sentiment to the design. And so Shadow Redwork™ was born. The bold graphic designs that nature provides for us coupled with subtle wording on the background (the shadow work) created an exciting effect. When my friend Todd Hensley (Publisher of C&T Publishing) saw the first few patterns he said we needed to do a book. One busy month of stitching the redwork with many loving hands made this book a reality. And so it is my pleasure to share these beautiful new designs with you. I hope you enjoy stitching your shadow redwork projects as much as I enjoyed designing them.

Happy stitching,
Alex

And so Shadow Redwork™ was born.

Nasturtiums Pillow

Size: 14¹/₂" x 17", design by Alex Anderson, redwork and pillow finishing by Nancy Sands.

See The Basics chapter beginning on page 39 for general instructions on how to create this pillow. Cut the background fabric 12¹/₂" x 15". Trim to 12" x 14¹/₂" after the stitching is complete. Use the Ruffle-Edge Pillow instructions on page 41 to complete the pillow.

Match the
dashed lines
to complete
the design.

See instructions
on pages 39-40.

Love Is Patient and Kind

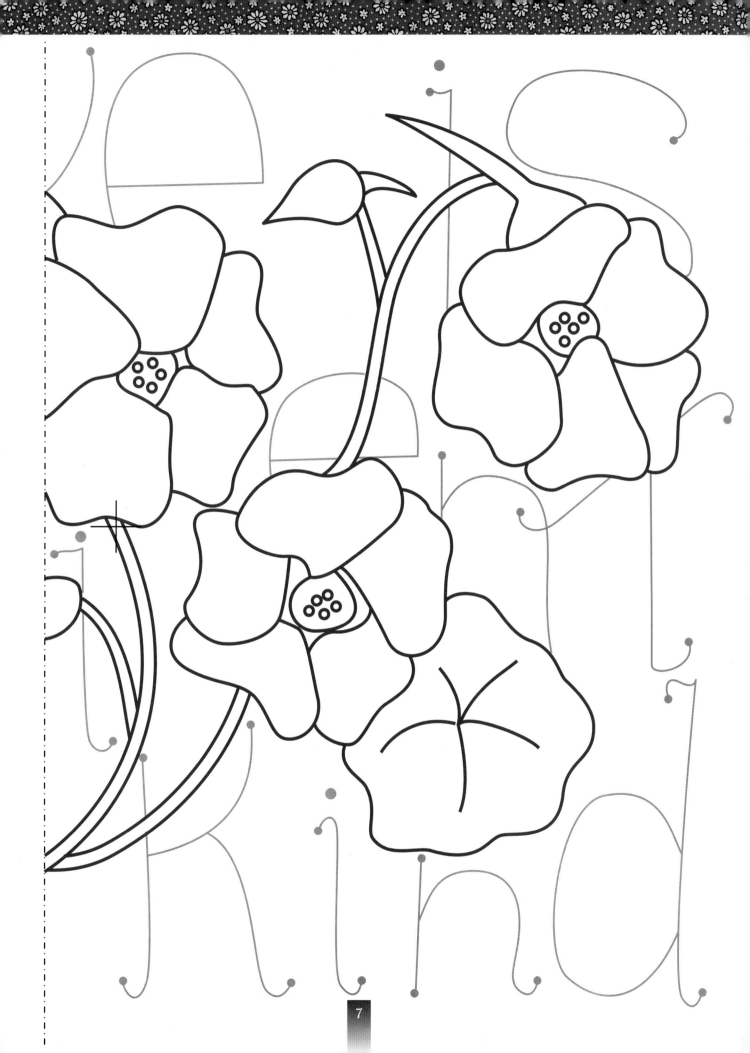

Sweet Peas Pillow

Size: 19" x 19", design by Alex Anderson, redwork and pillow finishing by Nancy Sands.

See The Basics chapter beginning on page 39 for instructions on how to enlarge the pattern and other general instructions for how to create this pillow. Cut the background fabric 16" x 16". Trim to 15 1/2" x 15 1/2" after the stitching is complete. Use the Flat Edge Pillow instructions on page 42 to complete the pillow.

Enlarge 200%, see instructions on page 39.

Fruit Quilt

Size: 29" x 29", design and machine quilting by Alex Anderson, redwork and piecing by Nancy Sands.

See The Basics chapter beginning on page 39 for general instructions on how to create this quilt. Cut the background fabric for each block 6½" x 6½". Trim to 6" x 6" after the stitching is complete. Cut six 1½" x 6" pieces for the short sashing strips, four 1½" x 19" pieces for the horizontal sashing strips, and two 1½" x 21" pieces for the vertical sashing. Cut two 4½" x 21" pieces for the top and bottom borders, and two 4½" x 29" pieces for the side borders. This quilt was quilted in-the-ditch (in the seamlines around all of the blocks, sashing, and borders).

See instructions on pages 39-40.

You shall eat the fruit...

See instructions on pages 39-40.

...of the labor of your hands.

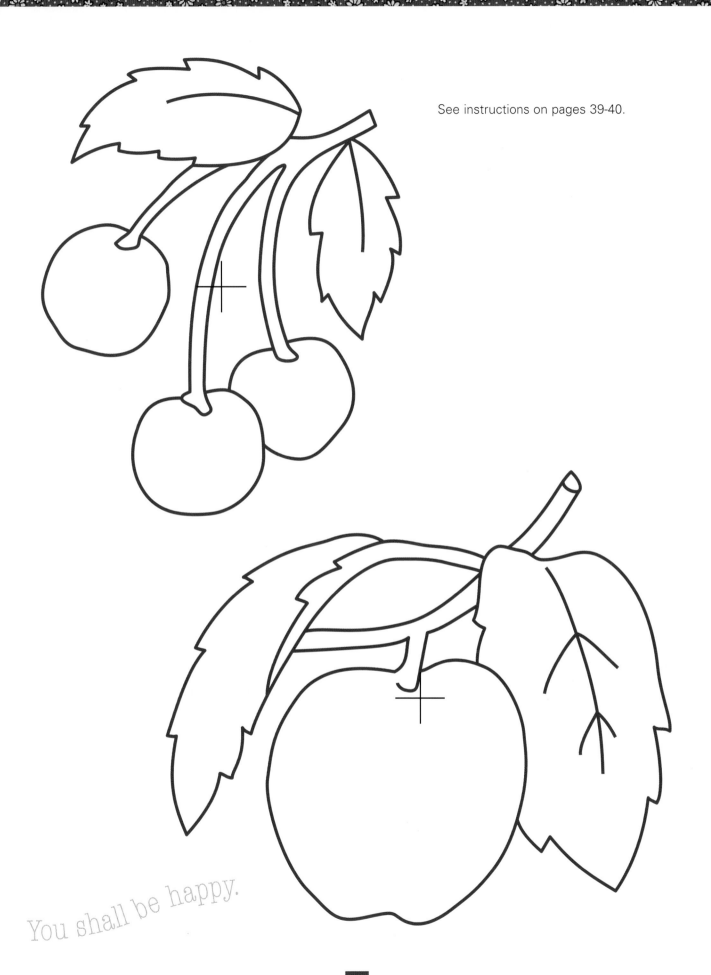

See instructions on pages 39-40.

You shall be happy.

See instructions on pages 39-40.

See instructions on pages 39-40.

Trace two and two
reversed for the corners.

You shall eat the fruit of the labor of your hands.

Match the dashed lines
to complete the design.

See instructions on
pages 39-40.

Match the dashed lines to complete the design.

See instructions on pages 39-40.

Match the dashed lines
to complete the design.

See instructions on
pages 39-40.

Match the dashed lines
to complete the design.

See instructions on
pages 39-40.

Love Hearts Quilt

Size: 45" x 45", design, piecing, and hand quilting by Alex Anderson, redwork by Pat Shaw.

See The Basics chapter beginning on page 39 for general instructions on how to create this quilt. Cut the background fabric for each block 16 1/2" x 16 1/2". Trim to 16" x 16" after the stitching is complete. See pages 43-44 for the pieced border instructions. This quilt was hand quilted. Notice that the lettering blends into the quilting when the quilting stitches cross the lettering stitches. If you want your lettering to stand out more, consider using a slightly darker thread color.

Framed Love Heart

Size: 24" x 24" including frame, design by Alex Anderson, redwork by Kimberly Watkins,
framed by Anna Pope of Proctor's Framing.

See The Basics chapter beginning on page 39 for general instructions. Cut the background fabric 16" x 16". Trim to 15½" x 15½" after the stitching is complete. Frame as desired.

Enlarge 200%, see instructions on pages 39-40.

Love binds everything together.

Enlarge 200%, see instructions on pages 39-40.

True love is the joy of life.

Enlarge 200%, see instructions on pages 39-40.

The aim of love is to love.

Enlarge 200%, see instructions on pages 39-40.

Love never claims, it ever gives.

Roses Wallhanging

Size: 19" x 24", design and finishing by Alex Anderson, redwork by Margaret Bender.

See The Basics chapter beginning on page 39 for general instructions on how to create this wallhanging. Cut the background fabric 16" x 21". Trim to 15$\frac{1}{2}$" x 20$\frac{1}{2}$" after the stitching is complete. Cut 2$\frac{1}{4}$" x 15$\frac{1}{2}$" pieces for the top and bottom border strips and 2$\frac{1}{4}$" x 20$\frac{1}{2}$" pieces for the side border strips. Cut four 2$\frac{1}{4}$" squares for the corners.

Enlarge 200%, see instructions on pages 39-40.

Some things have to be believed to be seen.

Bleeding Hearts Wallhanging

Size: 19" x 24", design and finishing by Alex Anderson, redwork by Pearl Denison.

See The Basics chapter beginning on page 39 for general instructions on how to create this wallhanging. Cut the background fabric 16" x 21". Trim to 15½" x 20½" after the stitching is complete. Cut 2¼" x 15½" pieces for the top and bottom border strips and 2¼" x 20½" pieces for the side border strips. Cut four 2¼" squares for the corners.

Enlarge 200%, see instructions on pages 39-40.

Keep your heart pure for from it flows the spring of life.

Daisies Wallhanging

Size: 19" x 24", design and finishing by Alex Anderson, redwork by Margaret Bender.

See The Basics chapter beginning on page 39 for general instructions on how to create this wallhanging. Cut the background fabric 16" x 21". Trim to $15^1/_2$" x $20^1/_2$" after the stitching is complete. Cut $2^1/_4$" x $15^1/_2$" pieces for the top and bottom border strips and $2^1/_4$" x $20^1/_2$" pieces for the side border strips. Cut four $2^1/_4$" squares for the corners.

Enlarge 200%, see instructions on pages 39-40.

Greatness is where simplicity, goodness & truth are found.

Fuchsias Wallhanging

Size: 19" x 24", design and finishing by Alex Anderson, redwork by Margaret Scott.

See The Basics chapter beginning on page 39 for general instructions on how to create this wallhanging. Cut the background fabric 16" x 21". Trim to 15½" x 20½" after the stitching is complete. Cut 2¼" x 15½" pieces for the top and bottom border strips and 2¼" x 20½" pieces for the side border strips. Cut four 2¼" squares for the corners.

Enlarge 200%, see instructions on pages 39-40.

Whatever is true, noble, right, pure & lovely, think on these.

Seasons Banner

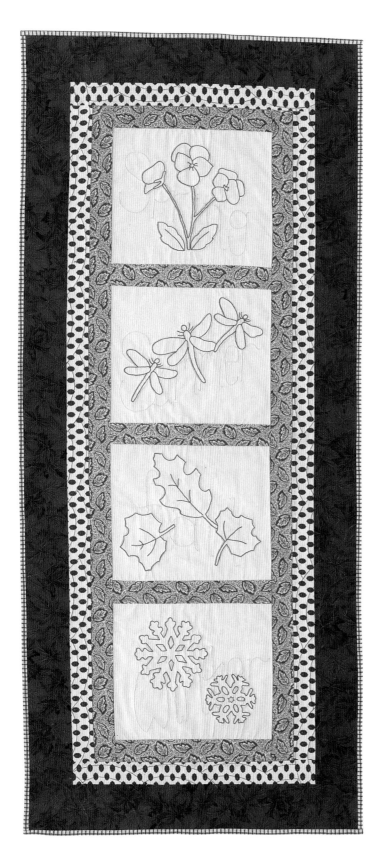

Size: 23$^1/_2$" x 53", design and finishing by Alex Anderson, redwork by Pearl Denison.

See The Basics chapter beginning on page 39 for general instructions on how to create this banner. Cut the background fabric for each block 12" x 10". Trim to 11$^1/_2$" x 9$^1/_2$" after the stitching is complete. Cut five 2" x 11$^1/_2$" pieces for the short sashing strips and two 2" x 44" pieces for the long sashing strips. Cut two 2" x 44" pieces for the side inner borders and two 2" x 17$^1/_2$" pieces for the top and bottom inner borders. Cut two pieces 3$^1/_2$" x 47" for the side outer borders and two pieces 3$^1/_2$" x 23$^1/_2$" for the top and bottom outer borders.

Spring

See instructions on pages 39-40.

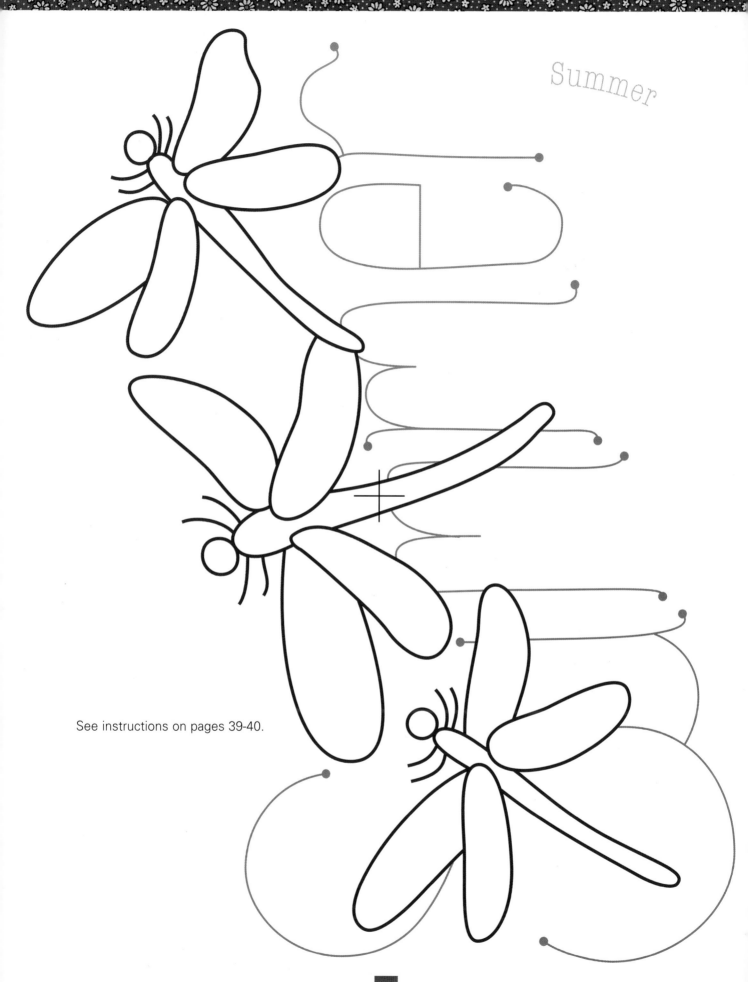

See instructions on pages 39-40.

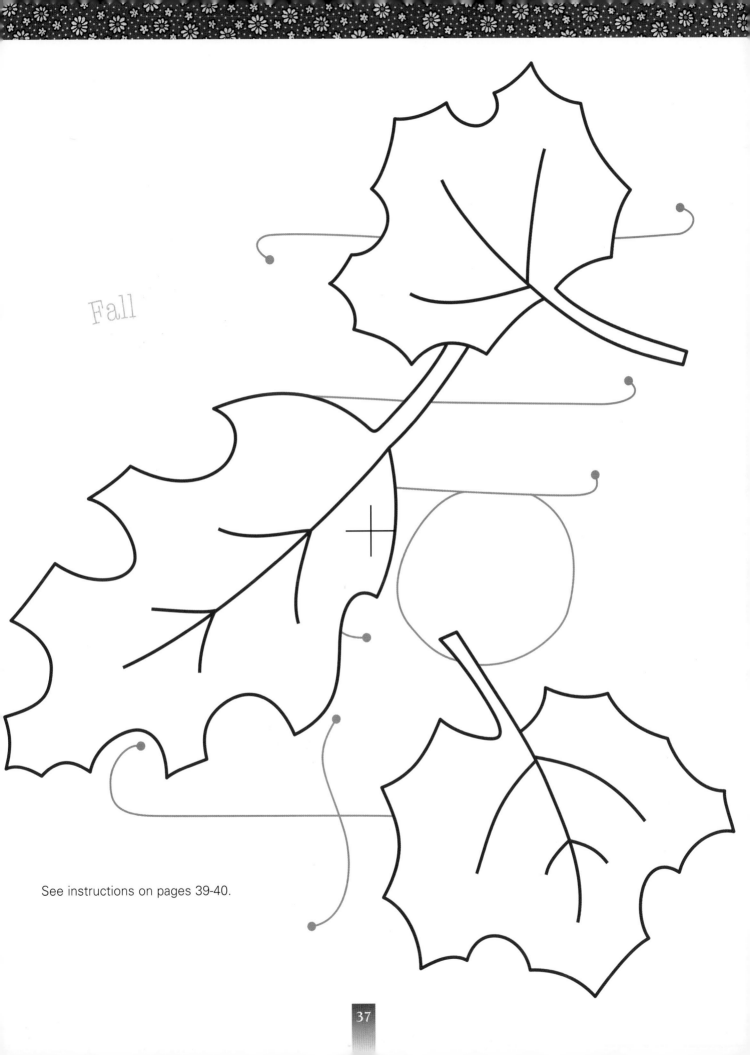

Fall

See instructions on pages 39-40.

Winter

See instructions on pages 39-40.

The Basics

Supplies

Fabric

Traditionally, redwork quilts were made using off-white or white cotton fabric for the background. There are wonderful 100% high-quality cottons currently on the market, as well as subtle prints, white-on-whites, tans, and tea-dyed cottons to choose from, depending on the look you want to achieve. I chose to work with Robert Kaufman's Kona cotton, the color snow, for a crisp look. I suggest that you pre-wash the fabric. If the fabric becomes too soft, use spray starch to regain the body.

There are great reproduction fabrics available to use for sashing and binding. When deciding on which fabric to use, make sure that the color matches or complements the red thread you are working with. If there is a substantial variation of color between the thread and accent fabric, your project may not be as successful as desired. Pre-wash or test the fabric for color migration, since the dyes used for red fabrics can cause problems.

Floss

Two strands of DMC six-ply embroidery floss (red #817 and ecru) were used for the projects shown in this book. Never use longer than an 18" length. Match the shadow work (lettering) color to the color of the background fabric you are using. If you are worried about color migration of the red thread, snip off a few inches and soak in hot water, then place them between two scraps of light-colored fabric on a non-porous surface (your kitchen counter). Cover with a non-porous object (cookie sheet or pie tin) and add a lightweight object (soup can) on top. Let it dry. If any color is left on the fabric, soak the floss in warm water until all color migration is gone, or simply discard the thread and use a different skein.

Tools

- ◆ Sharp embroidery needle
- ◆ Small embroidery hoop (I like to use a 4")
- ◆ Small, sharp scissors
- ◆ Extra-fine pencil
- ◆ Thimble

General Instructions

Enlarging the Patterns

Some of the patterns given need to be enlarged 200% on a photocopy machine to obtain the size needed. To accomplish this, photocopy half of the design (divided by a dashed line), enlarging by 200%, onto 11" x 17" paper. Repeat for the other half of the design. Tape the two halves of the pattern together matching the dashed lines.

Use the alphabet on pages 46 and 47 to create your own sentiments. Enlarge or reduce as needed.

Important Information

- ◆ The red lines indicate where to stitch the red floss; the gray lines indicate where to stitch the shadow work lettering.
- ◆ All measurements include ¼" seam allowances.
- ◆ Never "travel" thread between drawn lines and always trim any excess threads off the back to prevent them from showing through on the right side of the design.

1. Cut the background fabric pieces following the instructions given for the specific project.
2. Trace the pattern onto paper, if desired.
3. Center and pin the traced pattern underneath the fabric, using the + on the pattern to find the center.
4. Lightly trace only the redwork portion of the pattern. Position in a hoop and stitch.

5. After the redwork is completed, place it face down on a soft towel and press with an iron. The soft surface keeps the stitches from being crushed. Reposition the pattern on the fabric and trace the lettering (shadow work). You may need to make subtle adjustments. Again position in a hoop and stitch.

6. Press again after the block is completed, then trim to the size given.

Stitches

All the projects given in this book use three basic stitches: outline stitch, French knot, and lazy daisy. For the basic lettering use the outline stitch; for the dots and tails of letters, use the French knot; and on the fuchsias, a lazy daisy was used for the stamen.

Outline Stitch

Right-handed or left-handed: With a small knot in the end of the thread, bring the needle up through the fabric at #1 and pull the thread taut. Bring the needle down at #2 and up at #3 and pull the thread taut.

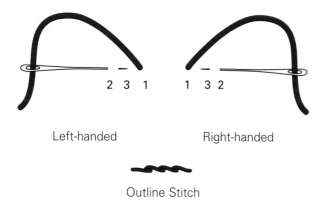

Left-handed   Right-handed

Outline Stitch

French Knot

With a small knot in the end of the thread, bring the needle up from the back of the fabric to the front of the fabric at #1 and pull it taut. Hold the thread taut and wrap the thread around the needle two or three times. Insert the needle back into the fabric at #2, just next to #1. Pull the thread taut.

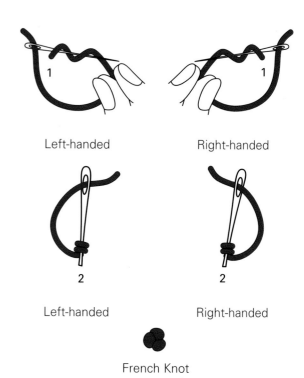

Left-handed   Right-handed

Left-handed   Right-handed

French Knot

Lazy Daisy

With a small knot in the end of the thread, bring the needle up from the back of the fabric to the front at #1 and pull it taut. Insert the needle down at #2, right next to where the thread came up through the fabric, and back up at #3 bringing the needle over the thread. Pull the thread taut. Bring the needle down at #4, making an anchor stitch.

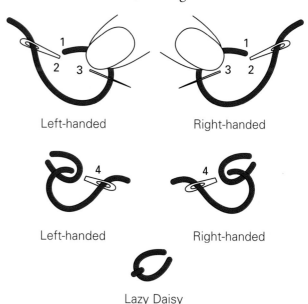

Left-handed   Right-handed

Left-handed   Right-handed

Lazy Daisy

Pillow Finishing

The following are general instructions for making the pillows shown in this book. You can adjust the numbers to create pillows from other projects shown. Adapt the cutting numbers to the appropriate size of your redwork piece. For a tightly stuffed pillow, cut the finished redwork piece 1" smaller than the pillow form. For example, if the pillow form is 14", the redwork piece should be 13" plus seam allowances.

Ruffle-Edge Pillow

1. Trim the redwork piece to the specified size.
2. Cut two pieces of fabric, the same size as the redwork piece. One is for the back of the pillow and the other is for the lining. Stitch the lining to the back of the redwork.
3. Red trim: Cut and piece 1"-wide strips of red fabric to at least 60" long. Fold lengthwise and press; it should measure $^1/_2$" by at least 60".
4. Beginning at the center bottom of the pillow, baste the red trim to the right side of the pillow top by hand or machine, raw edges together, using a $^1/_4$" seam allowance. Be sure to fold the beginning of the trim under to create a finished end. Stitch to within $^1/_4$" of the corner and backstitch. Fold the red trim up at a 45° angle, then down at a 90° angle to turn each corner. Start stitching at the edge (see illustration above right). Repeat for all four sides.

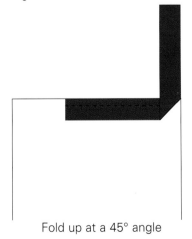

Fold up at a 45° angle

Fold down at a 90° angle.

5. Ruffle: Measure the outside edges of the pillow and double the number. Create a strip that is 3 $^1/_2$" by this measurement. Sew this strip into a continuous circle. Press the seam open. With wrong sides together, fold in half lengthwise and press. Sew two rows of gathering stitches.

Folded edge

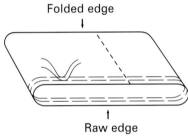

Raw edge

Sew into a continuous circle and sew gathering stitches.

6. Gather and pin evenly to the right side of the redwork, matching the raw edges. The ruffle should be facing the middle of the pillow. Stitch into place.

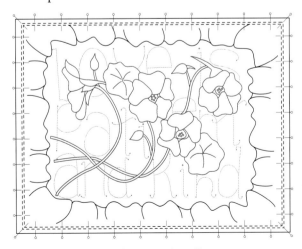

Pin the ruffle onto the pillow top.

7. Pillow Back: Pin the ruffle so it faces the center of the right side of the pillow top. Baste the backing onto the pillow top with right sides together.

8. Stitch with the redwork side of the pillow on top following the stitching lines of the red trim. Leave a 7" opening on the bottom edge to insert the pillow form. Backstitch at each side of the opening. Insert the pillow form and hand stitch the opening closed.

Note that the Nasturtiums Pillow is a rectangle. I used a square pillow form to give the pillow a nice tight look.

Flat-Edge Pillow

1. Trim the pillow top to the specified size.
2. Red trim: Cut and piece 1"-wide strips of red fabric to at least 64" long. Fold lengthwise and press; it should now measure $1/2$" by at least 64".
3. Beginning at the center bottom of the pillow, baste the red trim to the right side of the pillow top, by hand or machine, raw edges together using a $1/4$" seam allowance. Be sure to fold the beginning of the trim under to create a finished end. Before you approach each corner, fold the red fabric trim to turn each corner. See illustration on page 41.
4. Press the trim out, creating the look of a finished edge.
5. Pillow pocket: Measure the width of the pillow and add 4". Cut the pillow pocket fabric this measurement by the width of the fabric (42").
6. On the two short ends, fold the raw edges under $1/4$" twice, press, and stitch. You are creating a finished edge for the back pillow pocket opening.
7. Place the fabric rectangle on a table right side up. Fold the top down about two-thirds of the length of the pillow and then fold the bottom up about two-thirds of the length of the pillow. You are looking at the wrong side of the fabric. There will be an overlap in the middle of about 5".

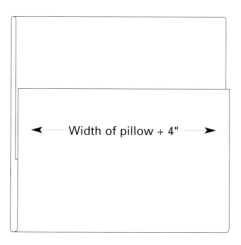

Width of pillow + 4"

Fold the fabric.

8. Center the prepared redwork on the fabric. Carefully adjust the folded fabric until you have 2" on all four sides of the redwork. When you get the desired size, remove the redwork and pin the raw edges. Sew the two raw edges using a $1/4$" seam allowance. Trim the seam allowance of the corners at a 45° angle for a clean sharp corner.
9. Turn the pillow pocket right side out and press.
10. Center the redwork pillow top on the completed pillow pocket. On the pillow back make sure the opening is horizontal and the top flap is facing down.
11. Carefully machine stitch the redwork picture onto the pillow pocket by stitching in-the-ditch along the red fabric trim.

Stitch-in-the-ditch

Quilt Construction

Sashing

1. Sew the blocks into rows with the short sashing strips between them.
2. Press the seams of each row alternating directions (e.g., row 1 left, row 2 right, and so on). This will allow you to easily align the seams when sewing the rows together. After the rows are sewn together, press the seams toward the sashing.
3. Sew the long sashing strips between the rows. Press.

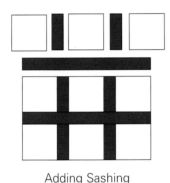

Adding Sashing

Borders

Plain Borders

If you want to add plain borders to any of the projects in this book, follow the instructions below.

1. Measure across the center of the redwork from side to side. Cut the top and bottom borders. Stitch these border strips to the top and bottom edges of the quilt top.
2. Measure the redwork across the center from top to bottom. Cut the side border strips this measurement by the width you desire (plus seam allowances). Stitch these border strips to the sides of the redwork.

Pieced Borders and Sashing

If you want to add pieced borders or sashing to any of the projects follow the instructions below, adjusting for the size of your blocks. Measurements given are for the *Love Hearts Quilt* (page 20).

1. For the pieced sashing: Cut 12 red strips 2" x 42" and 6 white strips 2" x 42". Sew a red strip on each side of one white strip (Strip Set 1). Press toward the red fabric. Repeat to make six strip sets.

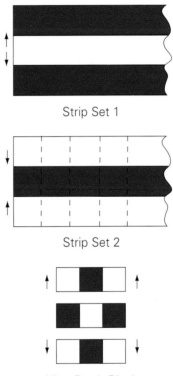

Strip Set 1

Strip Set 2

Nine-Patch Block

Cut the strip sets into:
   Twelve pieces 16" long (width of the block) for the sashing and borders
Save the leftovers for the Nine-Patches below.

2. For the Nine-Patch corner stones: Cut one red strip 2" x 42" and two white strips 2" x 42". Sew a white strip on each side of one red strip (Strip Set 2). Press toward the red fabric. Cut these strip sets into:
   Eighteen pieces 2" wide

From the leftover Strip Set 1 cut:
  Nine pieces 2" wide
Sew a Strip Set 2 piece on each side of one Strip Set 1 piece. Repeat to make nine Nine-Patch blocks.

3. Lay out the Redwork blocks, the sashing strips, and the Nine-Patch cornerstones following the photograph on page 20. Sew short sashing strips to the Redwork blocks to create horizontal rows. Press. Sew the Nine-Patch cornerstones to short sashing strips. Press. Sew these between the horizontal rows. Press.

Backing

Once you have finished your quilt top, it's time to consider the backing. If your quilt is wider than the standard 42", it will be necessary to piece the backing. When preparing the backing, here are thoughts to keep in mind:

✦ I used the same fabric for the backing as I used for the front. A darker fabric could show through, distorting the colors of the pieced top.

✦ Never use a sheet or designer fabric. It has a higher thread count and is difficult to hand quilt through.

✦ Always cut off the selvage edges before piecing the fabrics together—the seam might not lie flat.

✦ Always prewash the backing fabric and be sure it is a few inches larger on each side than the stitched piece, since it can shift during the quilting process.

Batting

For hand quilting I recommend using a low-loft polyester batting. For machine quilting I recommend you use 100% cotton batting. Make sure you follow the instructions if it needs to be prewashed.

Layering

Place the backing wrong side up. Carefully unroll the batting and smooth it on top of the backing. Trim the batting so it is about 2" larger on each side than the quilt top. Smooth the quilt top over the batting right-side up.

Basting

For Hand Quilting

Baste through all three layers in an approximately 4" grid pattern, so that there is an even amount of basting throughout the quilt. Never skimp on this part of the process; your quilt layers may slip and move during the quilting process.

For Machine Quilting

Pin baste every 3" with small safety pins. Pin evenly across the quilt, avoiding areas where the quilting stitches will be sewn.

Binding

The final step in constructing a quilt is the binding. Celebrate by using many different fabrics!

1. Trim the batting and backing even with the edges of the quilt top.
2. Cut the strips $2\frac{1}{8}$" (or a little wider if you prefer). If necessary piece the strips together with a diagonal seam, trim, and press open.

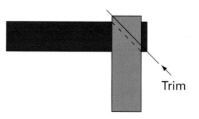

Piece with diagonal seams.

Press open.

3. Trim two of the strips the width of the quilt plus 1". Fold and press lengthwise.

Fold and press.

4. On the top edge of the quilt, align the raw edges of the binding with the raw edge of the quilt. Let the binding extend $1/2$" past the corners of the quilt. Sew using a $1/4$" seam allowance. Repeat for the bottom edge of the quilt.

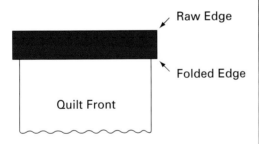

Raw Edge

Folded Edge

Quilt Front

Attach binding to front of quilt.

5. Bring the folded edge of the binding over the raw edges of the quilt and slipstitch to the back of the quilt. Trim the ends even with the quilt.

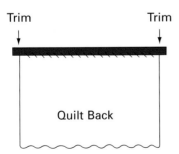

Trim   Trim

Quilt Back

Stitch binding and trim.

6. For the two sides of the quilt, cut the binding the length of the quilt plus $1/2$" for turning under. Fold over the two ends of the binding to create a finished edge and stitch. Again, turn the folded edge of the binding over the raw edge of the quilt and slip stitch into place.

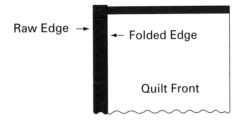

Raw Edge →   ← Folded Edge

Quilt Front

Attach side binding.

With the addition of a fabric label on the back to document your effort, your quilt is finished.

A B C D E F

G H I J K

L M N O P

Q R S T U

V W X Y Z

abcdefg
hijklmn
opqrstu
vwxyz12
3456789

About the Author

Alex's goal is to inspire and educate as many quilters as possible. Luckily, Alex is in a position to do just that. As host of HGTV's "Simply Quilts", she is well-known to the quilting community. Her award-winning quilts have been displayed at shows around the country for more than twenty years and widely published in books and magazines.

Alex describes her style of quiltmaking as "innovative-traditional." Her roots in the fine arts—she has a degree in art from San Francisco State University—and her deep appreciation for the work of quilters from past centuries have inspired her particular focus on fabric and color relationships along with traditional quilting designs.

Alex lives in northern California with her family. Visit her website at www.alexandersonquilts.com.

Other books by Alex Anderson

  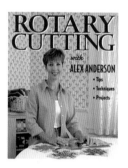  

For information about other C&T titles write for a free catalog:
C&T Publishing, Inc.
P.O. Box 1456
Lafayette, CA 94549
(800) 284-1114
e-mail: ctinfo@ctpub.com
website: www.ctpub.com

For quilting supplies:
Cotton Patch Mail Order
3405 Hall Lane, Dept. CTB
Lafayette, CA 94549
(800) 835-4418
(925) 283-7883
email: quiltusa@yahoo.com
website: www.quiltsusa.com